6

PERFORMANCE OF THE FEDERAL ENERGY OFFICE

Richard B. Mancke

NATIONAL ENERGY PROJECT

PERFORMANCE
OF THE FEDERAL
ENERGY OFFICE

Richard B. Mancke

American Enterprise Institute for Public Policy Research
Washington, D. C.

Richard B. Mancke is associate professor of international economic relations at the Fletcher School of Law and Diplomacy, Tufts University.

ISBN 0-8447-3150-1

National Energy Study 6, February 1975

Library of Congress Catalog Card No. 75-509

Printed in the United States of America

CONTENTS

THE AEI
NATIONAL ENERGY PROJECT

The American Enterprise Institute's
National Energy Project was established in early 1974
to examine the broad array of issues
affecting U.S. energy demands and supplies.
The project will commission research into all important
ramifications of the energy problem—economic
and political, domestic and international, private
and public—and will present the results
in studies such as this one.
In addition it will sponsor symposia, debates, conferences,
and workshops, some of which will be televised.

The project is chaired by Melvin R. Laird,
former congressman, secretary of defense,
and domestic counsellor to the President,
and now senior counsellor of *Reader's Digest*.
An advisory council, representing a wide range of
energy-related viewpoints, has been appointed.
The project director is Professor Edward J. Mitchell
of the University of Michigan.

Views expressed are those of the authors
and do not necessarily reflect the views of
either the advisory council and others associated with
the project or of the advisory panels,
staff, officers, and trustees of AEI.

PERFORMANCE OF THE FEDERAL ENERGY OFFICE

Introduction

Roughly 17 percent of the oil supplies for the United States were coming from Arab sources in late October 1973, when full-scale warfare again erupted on Israel's Egyptian and Syrian borders. Seeking to aid their Arab brethren, members of the Organization of Arab Petroleum Exporting Countries (OAPEC) unanimously agreed to reduce sharply—and, in the case of the United States and the Netherlands, eliminate totally—oil exports to countries that failed to adopt a "pro-Arab" foreign policy.[1] Because there were no substitutes for Arab oil readily available, the shortages precipitated by these actions threatened economic crisis.[2] In response, President Nixon

---

Discussions with Edward J. Mitchell, director of the AEI National Energy Project, and the comments and criticisms of three referees have helped to clarify several issues addressed in this paper. Responsibility for all conclusions remains the author's.

[1] OAPEC is composed of the Arab members of the Organization of Petroleum Exporting Countries (OPEC), which embraces all the major oil-exporting countries except Canada. Members of the OAPEC subgroup accounted for roughly 60 percent of OPEC's sales immediately before the start of the Arab embargo. The OAPEC members never explicitly defined a "pro-Arab" foreign policy. Their decision to embargo all sales to the United States and the Netherlands was apparently premised on the belief that these two countries were Israel's strongest supporters.

[2] Enormous geological variations distinguish oil and gas fields located in different parts of the world. Huge regional differences in the likely size, incidence, and productivity of petroleum sources explain the differences in the speed with which previously unplanned expansions in a region's oil output can take place. Specifically, because huge but undeveloped reserves of low-cost oil have already been discovered in such Persian Gulf countries as Iran, Kuwait, and Saudi Arabia, their output can be expanded merely by drilling the necessary additional wells and installing the appropriate surface gathering and storage facilities. Because of

issued an executive order establishing the Federal Energy Office (FEO), with instructions to initiate policies to alleviate the ill effects from domestic oil shortages. OAPEC officially ended its embargo of oil sales to the United States in mid-March 1974, and by mid-April U.S. petroleum supplies had been restored to adequate levels. The immediate crisis over, the FEO was replaced by the congressionally chartered Federal Energy Administration in early May.

The Federal Energy Office enjoyed a glamorous, hyperactive six-month existence. This paper constitutes a brief but comprehensive obituary evaluating its short lifetime. It deliberately departs from the customary eulogy in an effort to glean lessons for dealing with any future sudden interruptions in the supply of a key productive resource. Specifically, this evaluation concludes that, on balance, the measures taken by FEO actually exacerbated the nation's oil-supply problems. From this probe of the underlying causes of the FEO's policy failures, the most important lesson that emerges concerns planning. The oil shortages caused by the OAPEC embargo were severe enough that Americans somehow had to be persuaded to reduce their oil consumption. Even if the FEO had made no policy mistakes, cutbacks in oil consumption of the necessary magnitude inevitably would have been painful. Prior to the OAPEC embargo, the United States government had only the vaguest plans for dealing with such a contingency. Thus, both Congress and the White House panicked when it occurred. Good decision making is at best difficult in such a crisis atmosphere. It becomes nearly impossible when the organization responsible for making speedy decisions lacks adequate staff, administrative traditions, and a well-defined decision-making hierarchy, and is subject to political pressures from a plethora of interest groups. The blame for these deficiencies cannot be placed on the FEO. They were in fact inherent in its situation as a newly

---

the size and accessibility of these oil fields, only a one-year lag lies between a decision to expand future output from these sources and the production of significant quantities of that new output. In contrast, the location of large undeveloped oil fields in most non-Persian Gulf oil-producing countries is simply unknown. Hence, extensive exploration, which will take at least several years, is a necessary prerequisite for a large expansion of new oil supplies from these areas. In addition, because newly discovered oil fields in these areas will usually be much smaller, less productive, and less accessible than the new Persian Gulf fields, the time to develop them commercially is necessarily longer. For these reasons, the minimum lag between a decision to raise future crude-oil output appreciably above currently planned levels and the date when large amounts of this output will become available is now three to five years in areas like the U.S. Gulf of Mexico or the British North Sea and up to ten years in the Alaskan North Slope or northwestern Canada. Hence, worldwide oil shortages were an inevitable corollary of the OAPEC embargo.

established agency. It lies with Congress and, especially, the President, for failing to make adequate preparations to meet an oil embargo. Perhaps the government will have learned from the FEO's problems and formulate policies now for dealing with potential future interruptions of petroleum supplies.

1. Closing the Oil-Supply Gap

At birth, the most important problem facing the FEO was the need to prevent the United States from running out of oil. Realizing that substitutes for oil were not at hand, and not wishing to draw down inventories and bring on even worse shortages, the FEO responded with a conservation program initially designed to persuade, and if necessary to force, Americans to reduce their daily oil consumption by the entire 2.8 million barrels of crude oil or refined-product equivalents thought to come from Arab sources. The FEO pursued a two-pronged strategy. First, facing the possibility that other measures would fail, it started the extensive spadework for a rationing program that could force Americans to reduce their oil consumption by whatever amount might ultimately be necessary. Throughout December 1973 and early January 1974 this facet of the FEO's operations received the most public attention. It unleashed a flood of newspaper and television "special" reports detailing the difficulties commuters would suffer if rationing were imposed. Fortunately, the oil shortages were neither so prolonged nor so severe as to warrant rationing.

The second tactic employed by the FEO was to plead with consumers to accept voluntarily some hardship (in the form, for example, of lower temperatures in homes and offices and less pleasure driving) in order to reduce their petroleum demands. To put teeth into its pleas for "voluntary" conservation, the FEO persuaded Congress to force the states to return to daylight-saving time and (much more important) to cut maximum motor vehicle speeds.[3] It also relied on a mixed policy of persuasion and allocation regulations designed to result in sharp cutbacks in the quantities of oil products—especially gasoline—refiners could sell.

In late December, motorists in many urban areas began to endure hour-long waits to buy gasoline. Long lines at gas stations were to become the most visible and noxious symptom of the energy crisis in

---

[3] Year-round daylight-saving time directly conserved no appreciable amount of energy. However, it did serve to dramatize the severity of the energy crisis and thus probably encouraged greater voluntary conservation.

the United States.[4] In December the primary cause was panic buying. Many customers began "topping-out" their tanks with purchases of $1 or less because they feared more severe future shortages. As the lines began to lengthen, other motorists decided that they too should get into line. The panic was on.

The gas station lines were even longer and more widespread at the end of January and February 1974. By then, the reason was not topping-out, which most motorists realized was wasteful and time consuming, but the genuine shortages of gasoline at stations throughout the country. Misguidedly severe FEO policies imposed this painful, costly, and largely unnecessary symptom.

Table 1 presents monthly data on year-to-year changes in U.S. stocks of crude oil and refined products. These data establish that, on balance, the FEO's policies induced an overreaction to the Arab embargo. On the eve of the embargo (5 October 1973), although U.S. stocks of crude oil and all refined products except gasoline were slightly lower than the year before and most petroleum products were in tight supply,[5] no important sector of the economy was suffering from a severe shortage of petroleum products. Because U.S. petroleum consumption during the embargo averaged roughly 10 percent less than the year before, the FEO would not have been taking unnecessary risks if it had adopted measures that allocated petroleum products so that stocks always remained slightly below year-earlier levels.[6] Unfortunately, as Table 1 reveals, the FEO did not do this. Instead, by late April, when the embargo was lifted, stocks of every product except kerosene had registered significant improvement relative to the year before.

It is easy to calculate a rough quantitative estimate of the reduction in available petroleum supplies because higher stocks were accumulated. U.S. petroleum stocks totaled 848 million barrels at the onset of the OAPEC embargo, 27 million barrels, or 3 percent, below the year-earlier level.[7] However, by late April total stocks of

---

[4] See "FEO Seeks Relief on Crude Allocation," Oil and Gas Journal, 25 February 1974, p. 28.

[5] U.S. petroleum supplies had been tight throughout 1973. Prior to the Arab embargo too little refinery capacity was the cause of the supply stringency. For elaboration, see Richard B. Mancke, "Petroleum Conspiracy: A Costly Myth," Public Policy, Winter 1974, pp. 1–13.

[6] The use of year-to-year comparisons automatically takes account of the seasonal variations in inventories of most important petroleum products. To illustrate, oil companies typically build up large inventories of the distillate fuel oils used in space heating during the summer and draw them down during the winter.

[7] From the American Petroleum Institute's weekly refinery report, as reported in Oil and Gas Journal, 15 October 1973, pp. 180–81.

4

Table 1

YEAR-TO-YEAR CHANGES IN U.S. STOCKS OF CRUDE OIL AND REFINED PRODUCTS

(millions of barrels; percentage change in parentheses)

Period	Crude Oil (1)	Gasoline (2)	Jet Fuels (3)	Kerosene (4)	Distillate Fuel Oils (5)	Residual Fuel Oils (6)	Total Crude Oil and Products [a] (7)
Oct. 6, 1972 to Oct. 5, 1973	-10.80 (-4.2)	1.28 (0.6)	-5.95 (-19.7)	-0.73 (-3.3)	-0.29 (-0.1)	-7.90 (-12.3)	-26.87 (-3.1)
Nov. 3, 1972 to Nov. 2, 1973	-10.96 (-4.3)	2.92 (1.4)	-4.38 (-15.2)	1.86 (8.8)	6.81 (3.5)	-6.89 (-11.0)	-13.67 (-1.5)
Dec. 8, 1972 to Dec. 7, 1973	0.64 (0.2)	-6.72 (-3.1)	0.60 (2.2)	4.80 (24.1)	29.89 (16.8)	-0.83 (-1.5)	28.91 (3.4)
Jan. 12, 1973 to Jan. 11, 1974	1.23 (0.5)	-9.78 (-4.5)	3.35 (12.7)	4.20 (24.0)	44.66 (29.9)	-2.88 (-5.2)	43.69 (5.5)
Feb. 2, 1973 to Feb. 1, 1974	-4.96 (-2.1)	-3.83 (-1.7)	3.39 (13.4)	4.41 (27.5)	50.64 (38.4)	-2.85 (-5.8)	52.64 (6.8)
Mar. 2, 1973 to Mar. 1, 1974	0.89 (0.4)	9.79 (4.5)	4.42 (17.8)	2.16 (14.2)	36.54 (31.5)	-1.15 (-2.5)	58.22 (7.8)
Mar. 30, 1973 to Mar. 29, 1974	2.97 (1.2)	14.54 (6.8)	5.17 (19.6)	-1.21 (-6.9)	21.58 (19.5)	-1.47 (-3.2)	47.06 (6.2)
Apr. 27, 1973 to Apr. 26, 1974	7.39 (3.0)	20.48 (10.0)	4.30 (15.8)	-2.80 (-15.4)	18.36 (16.6)	1.76 (3.8)	51.85 (6.8)

[a] Includes aviation gas and unfinished oils, not shown separately.

Source: Raw data are from the American Petroleum Institute's weekly reports on stocks of crude oil and refined products as reported in the *Oil and Gas Journal*, October 1973–May 1974.

crude oil and refined products were up by nearly 7 percent, or about 52 million barrels, compared with a year earlier (see Table 1, column 7). This means that, precisely during the months of the Arab embargo, total U.S. petroleum inventories improved by about 80 million barrels when compared with the year-earlier date. The reduction in U.S. oil imports attributable to the embargo (assuming that they would have continued at October 1973 levels in its absence) was about 130 million barrels. However, because of the inventory build-up precipitated by the FEO's "successful" efforts to reduce the quantity of petroleum products available for sale, the effective short-fall suffered by American consumers was roughly 1.6 times that level—approximately 210 million barrels.

What might have happened if the Federal Energy Office had forced refiners to produce and offer for sale an additional amount of gasoline equivalent to the 80 million barrel net build-up of crude oil and refined product inventories that its actual policies fostered? According to Table 2, available U.S. gasoline supplies would have

---

Table 2

AVERAGE DAILY AVAILABLE SUPPLY, POTENTIAL SUPPLY, AND POTENTIAL DEMANDS OF GASOLINE IN THE UNITED STATES, JANUARY–APRIL 1974

(millions of barrels)

Month	Actual Available Supply[a]	Potential Available Supply[b]	Potential Demand Assuming No Embargo[c]	Excess of Potential Supply over Potential Demand
January	5.880	6.547	6.363	0.184
February	5.846	6.513	6.529	− 0.016
March	6.178	6.845	6.633	0.212
April	6.484	7.151	7.027	0.124

[a] Assumed to be equal to the sum of (1) average daily gasoline production by U.S. refiners, (2) average daily gasoline imports, and (3) the net reduction in gasoline inventories.

[b] Assumes that petroleum inventories were not built up relative to the preceding year during the embargo, and that, instead, refiners were forced to produce an additional 80 million barrels of gasoline which they made available for sale in January–April 1974.

[c] Assumes no shortages and prices remaining at pre-embargo levels. Calculated as equal to gasoline consumption in the corresponding month of 1973 plus 5 percent, the amount by which gasoline consumption in the first nine months of 1973 exceeded that in the corresponding period of 1972.

Source: Compiled from the weekly refinery reports of the American Petroleum Institute as reported in the *Oil and Gas Journal*, January 1974–May 1974.

averaged nearly 11 percent higher during January–April 1974, when gasoline was in tightest supply, if the FEO had encouraged oil refiners to maximize gasoline supplies while holding inventories of all petroleum products at their year-earlier levels. This "no-risk" allocation strategy would have totally eliminated the gap between potential gasoline demand (estimated assuming no embargo) and available supplies. In other words, the long lines at gas stations were not neccessary.

Why did the Federal Energy Office overreact to the OAPEC embargo? A key reason was its focus on the wrong variable—the anticipated reduction in U.S. oil imports—rather than on the level of U.S. petroleum stocks. Its anticipations proved to be exaggerated for two reasons. First, during the embargo the daily level of U.S. petroleum imports averaged more than 1 million barrels higher than the 2.8 million barrel cutback initially predicted, primarily because the international oil companies undertook the massive task of redirecting the world oil trade. In order to circumvent OAPEC's announced intention to impose the brunt of the embargo on the Netherlands and the United States, these companies began shipping to this country large quantities of non-Arab crude oil that normally would have gone elsewhere.[8] Moreover, because U.S. oil companies offered higher prices for them, imports of refined products did not fall by the amount predicted. In fact, for the first time in recent memory, high prices even pulled some gasoline and kerosene from the Soviet Union to the United States.

In addition to overestimating the cut in U.S. oil imports, the FEO did not take into account the indirect oil savings from the voluntary reduction in U.S. demand for two substitutes, coal and natural gas. For reasons elaborated upon shortly, substitution of the "saved" coal and natural gas curtailed demand for both distillate and residual fuel oils, which in turn staunched the drain on U.S. petroleum stocks.

2. Allocation Problems

The FEO correctly realized that the American people would embrace its voluntary conservation measures only if its allocation of the costs of the oil crisis was demonstrably fair. Hence, besides making sure that the United States did not run out of oil, the FEO's major duty

---

[8] At the start of the embargo some OAPEC members (notably Libya) continued to ship some oil to the United States. Unfortunately, this information was leaked to the press by government officials, after which the flow of "hot" OAPEC oil dried up immediately. Source: interviews with former FEO officials.

was to develop and implement policies to spread the burdens of petroleum shortages in an efficient and equitable way.[9] Seeking to do this, the FEO introduced allocation measures designed to place a heavier burden on users thought to be better able to reduce their consumption without severe economic disruption (for example, most industries, but apparently not petrochemicals and trucking) or in some vague ethical sense less deserving (for example, motorists).[10] Unfortunately, even ignoring the complaints from each group that believed its share of the burden was unconscionably high, the FEO soon found that just and efficient allocation was no easy task. Four of its allocation problems are discussed below.

Allocation between Gasoline and Distillate Fuel Oil. Gasoline and distillate fuel oils are quantitatively the two most important refined-oil products. Most gasoline is used to power motor vehicles; most distillates are consumed either in industrial and home heating or in fueling diesel engines. U.S. gasoline consumption averaged 6.6 million barrels per day in 1973; the consumption of distillates averaged 3.2 million barrels.

Because, during winter, adequate home heating is obviously much more important to human life than most automobile travel, the FEO concluded that Americans would find it least disruptive to reduce their consumption of gasoline proportionately more than their consumption of distillate fuel oils. Hence, it repeatedly exhorted refiners to produce more distillate oils and less gasoline. Besides exhortation, it employed the price-setting powers delegated to it by the Cost of Living Council to skew allowable refined-product prices so that distillate sales were more profitable than gasoline sales. Table 1 confirms that by early December 1973 stocks of distillate fuel oils far exceeded year-earlier levels. But simultaneously, those notorious gasoline lines were beginning to form. The FEO had overestimated

---

[9] For reasons discussed below, the legislation authorizing petroleum allocation was actually written several months before the OAPEC embargo. Hence, a reading of the legislation does not suggest that the goal of allocation was to spread the burdens of the petroleum shortage in an efficient and "equitable" way. Nevertheless, after the embargo, this should have been the FEO's goal.

[10] No objective definition of an equitable distribution of the burdens of petroleum shortages is possible. Most individuals define as equitable all redistributions that benefit them. During the OAPEC embargo those interest groups with the most political clout tended to receive favored treatment. Thus, farmers and truckers were awarded higher allocations of petroleum products than less vocal consumers, and some refiners were subsidized by being granted the right to buy "cheap" crude oil from their competitors (of which more below). See "FEO Revises Allocation Rules Again," *Oil and Gas Journal*, 21 January 1974, p. 38.

the supply problems for distillate fuel oil and underestimated those for gasoline.

Even so, until late January 1974, the FEO continued to urge refiners to produce more distillates at the expense of gasoline, and until mid-February it manipulated price ceilings to achieve this end. The burgeoning distillate inventories—they had soared to more than 38 percent above year-earlier levels by early February—spurred by this policy are plainly illustrated in Table 1. If the FEO had instead adopted policies that required refiners to maintain distillate stocks at corresponding year-earlier levels, daily U.S. gasoline production could have averaged 403,000 barrels (or 6.5 percent) higher during the first four months of the OAPEC embargo (see Table 3).

Three factors explain why the FEO's emphasis on distillate fuel oils proved to be misplaced. First was a fortuitous warm winter in the more populous eastern half of the country. Second, in our car-dependent society, most motorists were unwilling to make the significant changes in life style that would have brought about immediate reductions in car miles traveled until they were forced to do so by "gasless" Sundays, alternate-day rationing, and the impossibility of

Table 3

AVERAGE DAILY U.S. PRODUCTION OF GASOLINE, ACTUAL AND POSSIBLE, OCTOBER 1973 THROUGH JANUARY 1974

(millions of barrels)

Month	Actual[a]	Possible[b]	Excess of Possible over Actual (percent)
October	6.551	6.794	3.7
November	6.395	7.055	10.3
December	6.080	6.502	6.9
January	5.883	6.168	4.8
Four-month average	6.227	6.630	6.5

[a] Given FEO policies.

[b] Calculated by assuming that without the special encouragement that distillate production received from FEO policies, U.S. refiners would have produced sufficient amounts of distillate fuel oils to maintain stocks at corresponding year-earlier levels, and that any crude oil made available as a result of this decision was refined into gasoline.

Source: Compiled from the American Petroleum Institute's weekly refinery reports as reported in the *Oil and Gas Journal*, October 1973–February 1974.

finding fuel. Even when they were willing, changing ingrained driving habits that resulted in high gas consumption required constant vigilance. In contrast, significant reductions in demands for distillate fuel oils followed directly from some extremely simple moves. Most obvious, in northern climes use of fuel oil for heating could be cut back 6 to 10 percent merely by turning down thermostats 6 degrees. Third, because Americans voluntarily reduced their demands for coal and natural gas (which together supply roughly 50 percent of total U.S. energy needs) by about 10 percent below predicted nonembargo levels, some industrial consumers who normally used distillate fuel oil could turn to these other fuels. To illustrate, in recent years U.S. supplies of natural gas have been inadequate to satisfy winter heating demands.[11] Therefore, many industrial, commercial, and institutional users buy natural gas on interruptible contracts and expect their supplies to be stopped during winter. When this happens, most do not shut down but, instead, begin burning other fuels, including distillate or residual fuel oils. The voluntary cutbacks by natural-gas users during winter 1973–74 reduced the number and duration of natural-gas interruptions, thus lightening demands for distillate fuels. Because most automobiles are powered by gasoline, no comparable reduction was experienced in gasoline demand.

Interregional Allocation of Gasoline. Some sections of the country are much more dependent on oil imports than others. On the eve of the OAPEC embargo, well over half of the Northeast's oil demands were being supplied from foreign sources other than Canada. In stark contrast, the Gulf Coast states and their immediate neighbors had access to domestic supplies sufficient to meet all their needs. Obviously, after the onset of the embargo, both efficiency and equity made it desirable to reallocate large quantities of oil from relatively oil-rich to relatively oil-poor regions.[12]

Gasoline was the petroleum product in tightest supply throughout the Arab embargo. In order to ensure that the available supplies would be distributed equitably around the country, the FEO issued

---

[11] Inadequate natural gas supplies are the direct result of wellhead price regulation of natural gas sold in interstate markets by the Federal Power Commission. Most oil economists agree that holding the price of natural gas below market-clearing levels is one of the most costly of U.S. energy policies. For elaboration see Edward Mitchell, *U.S. Energy Policy: A Primer* (Washington, D. C.: American Enterprise Institute, 1974), pp. 53–69.

[12] Congressional representatives of the oil-poor regions used every political resource at their command to force the FEO to get them a larger share of the total U.S. petroleum supplies.

regulations requiring that, after meeting certain priority needs (trucking and farming, for example), oil companies had to allocate their gasoline among their dealers according to sales in the corresponding month of 1972. (The reasons for basing allocations on 1972 sales will be discussed shortly.)

The FEO regulations did not, however, achieve equitable interstate distribution of gasoline supplies. As Table 4 shows, in February, when gasoline shortages were most severe, initial allocations for the states ranged from a low of 63 percent of projected needs in both New Hampshire and Virginia to a high of 122 percent of projected needs in Wyoming. States that produced large quantities of oil or bordered oil-exporting western Canada had the most gasoline so that most of their residents suffered no direct discomfort from the embargo. Hardest hit were five eastern states (New Hampshire, New Jersey, Vermont, Virginia, and West Virginia), whose initial allocations averaged only 66 percent of their projected needs. Even after these states were awarded emergency supplementary allocations in late February, their available supplies averaged only 73 percent of projected needs. Obviously, in these and similarly situated states, stringent belt-tightening was necessary to reduce gasoline consumption to the low level of available supplies. And even that was not enough; large areas of most of these states completely ran out of gasoline at the end of both January and February.

Transportation bottlenecks were probably the chief cause of the large interstate differences in gasoline supply: the network of petroleum-product pipelines in the United States did not have sufficient extra capacity to ship the necessary quantities of gasoline from relatively gasoline-rich to relatively gasoline-poor regions. Apart from this physical limitation, the allocation regulation itself helped to exaggerate shortages in three ways:

1. Basing allocations on 1972 sales disproportionately hurt fast-growing regions such as Arizona, Florida, and Nevada.[13]

2. In 1972 major oil companies (British Petroleum, Gulf, Phillips) began consolidating retailing operations by closing several

---

[13] The FEO allowed gas stations that desired more gasoline than they were allotted by the general allocation rule because of special circumstances (for example, a sharp jump in their sales volume had occurred since the 1972 base period) to file "Form 17s." Thousands were filed. Unfortunately, inadequate staffing prevented the FEO from processing most of them. Hence, few exceptions were granted prior to March. The FEO decided to honor all Form 17 requests in March. As a result, by April the interregional allocation program for gasoline stations had been effectively gutted. Since the gasoline shortage was over, this was a desirable result. Source: interviews with former FEO officials.

Table 4

FEBRUARY GASOLINE ALLOCATIONS, BY STATE

(millions of gallons)

State	Projected February Need	Initial February Supply	Supply as Percent of Need	Emergency February Allocation	Initial plus Emergency Allocation as Percent of Need
Wyoming	17.6	21.5	122	—	—
Louisiana	141.3	154.0	109	—	—
Kansas	99.0	106.9	108	—	—
Minnesota	159.9	164.7	103	—	—
Oklahoma	118.9	121.3	102	—	—
Texas	548.2	542.7	99	—	—
Hawaii	22.3	21.4	96	—	—
Arkansas	86.2	82.8	96	—	—
New Mexico	48.9	46.5	95	—	—
Colorado	105.4	99.1	94	—	—
Alaska	8.8	8.3	94	—	—
North Dakota	25.1	23.3	93	—	—
Idaho	32.5	29.9	92	—	—
Maine	37.5	34.1	91	3.4	100
Washington	123.1	112.0	91	—	—
Nebraska	66.8	59.5	91	—	—
Delaware	22.8	20.3	89	2.0	98
D.C.	18.7	16.6	89.	1.7	98
Massachusetts	184.9	162.2	88	16.2	97
New York	465.1	409.3	88	40.9	97
Michigan	343.4	295.3	86	—	—
Utah	44.7	38.0	85	—	—
California	791.4	672.7	85	—	—
South Dakota	31.0	26.4	85	—	—
Ohio	397.9	319.1	84	—	—
Tennessee	176.2	148.0	84	14.8	92
Wisconsin	162.9	135.2	83	—	—
Montana	33.0	27.4	83	—	—
Kentucky	126.2	103.5	82	10.4	90
Rhode Island	35.7	29.3	82	1.9	87
Florida	362.0	293.2	81	17.6	86
Iowa	123.5	100.0	81	—	—
Mississippi	97.2	78.7	81	7.9	89
South Carolina	112.1	90.8	81	9.0	89
North Carolina	214.9	171.9	80	17.2	88
Indiana	210.6	166.4	79	16.6	87
Missouri	199.0	155.2	78	15.5	86
Connecticut	112.4	87.7	78	8.8	86
Illinois	407.3	313.6	77	31.4	85
Pennsylvania	401.7	305.3	76	30.5	84
Maryland	146.8	110.1	75	11.0	82

Oregon	91.5	67.7	74	6.8	81
Alabama	143.4	104.7	73	10.5	80
Arizona	101.5	73.1	72	7.3	79
Georgia	242.9	174.9	72	—	—
Nevada	27.4	19.2	70	1.9	77
New Jersey	307.8	212.4	69	21.2	76
Vermont	19.6	13.5	69	1.4	76
West Virginia	58.6	39.3	67	3.9	74
New Hampshire	31.1	19.6	63	2.0	69
Virginia	233.0	146.8	63	14.7	69

Source: *National Journal Reports*, 9 March 1974. From data used by the Federal Energy Office.

thousand stations in regions of the country where inadequate or obsolete refining capacity made retailing relatively less profitable. Normally these oil companies might have been expected to build new refineries to supply these markets at less cost. However, because oil import quotas were still in effect, builders of new refineries had no guarantee of securing the necessary supplies of crude oil; prudence thus dictated that no new refineries be built.[14] Abandonment of gas stations was especially prevalent in the Southeast and Midwest. Since each oil company's available gasoline was to be allocated on the basis of its dealers' 1972 sales, these areas suffered a disproportionate fall in gasoline supplies.[15]

3. Like states, oil companies relied on imported oil in widely varying degree. Domestic crude-oil supplies of companies like Exxon, Getty, Gulf, and Marathon were sufficient to supply most of their refineries' needs. In contrast, the embargo led to proportionately larger falls in output for companies like Ashland and Sohio. Those states (chiefly on the East Coast) with heavy concentrations of stations supplied by these refineries thus suffered more than others.

In addition to failing to correct the sharp inequities among states, the FEO's program also led to misallocation of gasoline supplies within states. The long lines that were commonplace in most major eastern urban centers from late December 1973 through February 1974 were unknown in many rural and vacation areas located in the same states. Urban areas suffered most because throughout the

---

[14] This disincentive was eliminated in May 1973, when the President issued an executive order abolishing the United States's Mandatory Oil Import Quota Program. By this time, several oil companies had already closed down retailing operations in large regions of the country.

[15] Some dealers who had gone out of business after 1972 found that it was profitable to reopen during the OAPEC embargo. The allocation regulations required their former suppliers to resupply them. Source: interviews with former FEO officials.

embargo drivers tended to fill their tanks close to home or work. The sharp reductions in pleasure driving and weekend trips meant that far fewer fill-ups took place in outlying rural and vacation areas.

Despite the good intentions of the FEO program to allocate available gasoline supplies equitably among regions, it failed. Enormous interregional differences in gasoline supplies persisted throughout the embargo. A better policy would have allowed oil companies to charge slightly higher prices on sales to dealers in areas classified by the FEO as gasoline-short. Since the FEO's price controls on petroleum products did take account of interregional differences in gasoline production and delivery costs, allowing oil refineries to impose a surcharge of about 1¢ per gallon on sales in gasoline-short areas should have provided ample incentive for the elimination of the costly regional shortages.

Intertemporal Allocation of Gasoline. One of the most frustrating problems posed by the Arab embargo was the worsening of gasoline shortages near the end of the month. These intertemporal supply inequities created wasteful end-of-the-month transportation bottlenecks in most regions of the country. Paradoxically, these cyclical shortages arose largely from one of the FEO's pricing regulations: the decision to allow refiners and dealers to raise prices to offset higher costs only at the start of each month. With costs of gasoline production soaring, this rule gave refiners a strong incentive to withhold gasoline at the end of a month for sale at the beginning of the new month, when they could charge the new higher price.[16]

The gasoline shortages were especially severe at the end of February, when many eastern motorists found it impossible to purchase any gasoline.[17] The blame rests squarely on the FEO announcement in mid-February that gas stations would be allowed to raise their margins from 8¢ to 10¢ on each gallon sold after 1 March. A dealer's profit-maximizing response to such an announcement would be to lock up his station until March. Many did just that.

The American motorists' monthly cycle of relative feast followed by absolute famine could have been largely eliminated by allowing oil companies to pass through higher costs as they occurred and by allowing dealers to raise their margins on the date the rule change was announced.

---

[16] To illustrate, because of higher raw material costs, most refiners were allowed to raise their prices by about 4¢ per gallon on 1 March. Therefore, they held back on late February deliveries.

[17] Source: interviews with former FEO officials.

14

Interrefinery Allocation of Crude Oil. American oil companies depend on Arab crude in widely varying degree. Those that were most dependent, and therefore faced the severest shortages, persuaded Congress that this situation was not equitable. The Federal Energy Office was therefore instructed by Congress to establish a program requiring relatively crude-rich refiners to share supplies with their less fortunate competitors. To implement this directive, the FEO (as of 1 February 1974) ordered refiners with crude-oil supplies that exceeded the industry average to sell some of their "surplus" to crude-poor competitors. The maximum price a refiner could charge for its "surplus" was set equal to the weighted average of its total crude-oil costs from all sources. Because most price-controlled domestic crude cost several dollars less per barrel than foreign crude, crude-poor refiners like Ashland and Sohio found that they could reduce their costs by curtailing their own imports of non-Arab oil at $10.00-plus per barrel and, instead, buying "surplus" from crude-rich refiners like Exxon and Gulf for about $7.00. For the same reason, crude-rich refiners realized they would lose several dollars on every barrel of oil imported and then sold at the maximum average price. The regulation thus had the perverse effect of encouraging both crude-short and crude-rich refiners to cut back their oil imports.

To soften the impact on crude-rich refiners who were forced to sell crude to others, the FEO issued three regulations. First, the "84¢ provision" allowed them to raise their refined-product prices enough to capture an additional 84¢ of revenue for each barrel they sold. Second, they could add a 6 percent selling fee to their average crude-oil costs before making any sales to their crude-short competitors. Third, they could raise their prices for petroleum products by an amount equal to the reduction in their profits caused by the forced sale.[18] Taken together, these three supplementary regulations allowed crude-rich refiners to more than recover their total "losses" (that is, their potential but unrealized profits) due to forced sales. As a result, imports did not decline appreciably because of the FEO's interrefinery allocation regulations. In September 1974, John Sawhill, then head of the Federal Energy Administration, accused the crude-rich refiners that took advantage of all three supplementary regulations of "double-dipping" because they recovered more than 100 percent of the reduction in their profits due to the forced sales of their crude oil and in

---

[18] This clause read: "Refineries required to sell crude oil under this program shall be allowed to increase their product prices to reflect increased crude oil cost of all available crude prior to making crude oil sales to comply with this program." Reprinted in "Double-Dipping Oil Companies?" *Wall Street Journal*, 17 September 1974, p. 22.

the process overcharged consumers by $100 million to $300 million.[19] Sawhill's criticism was too strong. First of all, the FEO staff became aware of the possibility of double-dipping only when top officials of several major oil companies told them about it.[20] Second, many oil companies refrained from exercising their legal right to double-dip, so that the "overcharge" was probably far less than Sawhill's initial estimate.[21] Third, the possibility of double-dipping arose only because the FEO established a cumbersome, poorly designed interrefinery allocation program that required complicated special exemptions to forestall severe disincentives to import oil.

Who Was Responsible for the Allocation Failures? The policies of the FEO did not achieve a just and efficient petroleum allocation among products, regions, refiners, or time periods. Many have charged the oil companies with the responsibility for these failures. After all, their indictment reads, if the companies had not reached greedily for higher profits, the observed misallocation of petroleum supplies need not have been so severe. As the foregoing discussion amply documents, however, if the oil companies were at fault, it was because they responded in accordance with the price controls, the regulatory constraints, and the repeated public pleas of the FEO. Indeed, they would have deserved the strongest public censure if they had done otherwise during a period of national economic crisis.

At least some of the responsibility for the FEO's misguided allocation measures rests with the Congress whose Emergency Petroleum Allocation Act called for a comprehensive allocation program within thirty days of its passage. Though passed in November 1973, after the OAPEC embargo was imposed, this act had been drafted six months earlier. At that time Congress perceived two chief energy problems: (1) inadequate supplies of crude oil for independent refiners, who bought most of their crude oil inputs, and (2) inadequate supplies of petroleum products for independent dealers, who since early 1973, had been cut off by refiners suffering from a shortage of refinery capacity. In order to satisfy the intent of Congress to aid the independent dealers and its instructions to base allocations on more "normal" 1972 conditions, the FEO geared its gasoline allocation

---

[19] See "Allocation Bungle Triggers FEA Probe," *Oil and Gas Journal*, 23 September 1974, p. 112.

[20] Source: interviews with former FEO officials and "FEA Bungling," *Wall Street Journal*, 8 October 1974, p. 28.

[21] A subsequent estimate of the actual overcharge was $40 million. See "FEA Bans Costs Pass-through via 'Double Dip,'" *Oil and Gas Journal*, 7 October 1974, p. 54.

measures to customer-supplier relationships in that year. Unfortunately, these had changed drastically by early 1974 because many independents, unable to get adequate supplies, had lost sales, acquired new suppliers, or left the business. Given the haste with which the FEO was created, its staff lacked both the size and the expertise to implement the complex and highly detailed measures necessary for adjusting to these changes. Many of these administrative problems persisted until April, when the embargo was over. If Congress had given the FEO greater administrative flexibility, many could have been avoided and the allocation measures might have proven more successful.[22]

3. Price Controls

No evidence has been presented to support the widely held belief that the large oil companies engineered the petroleum shortages during the OAPEC embargo in order to reap sharply higher profits. Nevertheless, the mere fact that so many Americans held it meant that their cooperation with the FEO's voluntary conservation plans depended on confidence in FEO's efforts to prevent profiteering from the shortage. The FEO used the price-setting powers delegated to it by the Cost of Living Council in this effort. They failed. Understanding how and why requires some background.[23]

Multi-tiered Prices for U.S. Crude Oil. Domestic crude-oil prices were rising in early 1973. As part of its program to combat inflation and to prevent owners and producers of previously developed supplies from reaping windfall profits, the Cost of Living Council set ceiling prices on all crude oil classified as "old"—that from leaseholds producing prior to 1973. The council believed that this action would not lead to reduced production of old oil because the out-of-pocket costs of exploiting most developed sources were far lower than the ceiling price. However, responding to pressure from politically powerful owners, Congress exempted the oil from low-productivity stripper wells that produced less than 10 barrels of crude oil per day. Stripper oil pro-

---

[22] One caveat is necessary. Some lawyers familiar with the Emergency Petroleum Allocation Act have told the author that they feel the FEO's interpretation of its powers was far too narrow.

[23] A more comprehensive discussion of price controls on oil may be found in William A. Johnson, "The Impact of Price Controls on the Oil Industry: How to Intensify an Energy Crisis," George Washington University, 1974 (unpublished).

duction costs were already near the May ceiling price and rising sharply due to the rapid price inflation of drilling equipment and supplies. Hence, the justification for the exemption ran, imposition of effective price ceilings would perversely discourage output, precisely at a time of tight supply, by making it unprofitable to continue producing from marginal fields, to rework closed fields, and to make the investment necessary for boosting output from stripper wells already in operation.

The Cost of Living Council also recognized that higher crude prices would encourage oil companies to expand greatly their investments for exploration and for developing and producing oil from new sources. Hence, "new" crude—production from a leasehold above the level achieved in 1972—was also exempted from the price ceilings. To reinforce these incentives, a barrel of "released" crude was also exempted from the price ceilings each time a barrel of new crude was produced. As of mid-June 1974, approximately 40 percent of all U.S.-produced crude oil was exempt from price controls.

Before the imposition of price controls, the price paid by oil refiners for any specified barrel of crude oil corresponded directly with its economic value. Thus, premiums were paid for (1) higher-gravity crudes because they yield proportionately more gasoline, (2) low-sulphur crudes because they are cheaper to refine and their products contain fewer pollutants and therefore are more valuable, and (3) crudes located relatively close to major refining and consuming centers. Since the imposition of controls, the price paid for a barrel of crude oil delivered to any specified American refinery has also depended on whether it is classified as old, exempt (that is, new, released, or stripper oil), foreign, or some combination of the three. Old oil is cheapest. Its average wellhead price has been $5.25 per barrel since late 1973. In sharp contrast, exempt oil of similar quality has been selling for about $10.00, and in early 1974 most foreign oil delivered to U.S. refineries ranged between $10.00 and $15.00 per barrel.[24]

Unlike stripper oil and new oil, production of discovered and developed old oil is not likely to be very price-responsive (in the vicinity of present prices) except over a span of several years.[25] Hence, assuming that the price controls on this product would be

---

[24] See "U.S. Exempt-oil Prices May Stall at $10/bbl. Level," *Oil and Gas Journal*, 4 February 1974, p. 34; "U.S. Crude Price Rollback Seen Certain," *Oil and Gas Journal*, 18 February 1974, p. 46.

[25] There is one exception to this rule. Large annual expenditures are necessary to maintain oil output from most oil fields where secondary recovery is being used. Hence, the supply of old oil from these fields is probably relatively price responsive.

short-lived, the Cost of Living Council (and subsequently the FEO) was probably correct in inferring that they would not lead to an appreciable reduction in supply.

Well before the start of the Arab embargo, the shortages that developed made it evident that the price ceilings on old oil had been set far below market-clearing levels. Crude-short refiners, desperate for refinery feedstocks, bid up the price of exempt crude. Desiring even more oil, they began seeking ways to circumvent the price controls of old oil. According to reports in the trade press prior to the OAPEC embargo, some succeeded by agreeing to tie together purchases of old and new oil from a given source: they bought old oil at the controlled price, but bought new oil at a price so high that the weighted average price for the total purchase rose to near the market-clearing level.[26] Thus, the price controls on old oil had the undesirable consequence of accelerating the inflation of prices of new oil.

U.S. petroleum supplies became much tighter after the OAPEC embargo. Realizing that producers of old oil would almost certainly require tie-in purchases in order to circumvent the price controls, the FEO froze all buyer-seller arrangements on old oil as of 1 December 1973. This ruling eliminated the possibility of tie-in sales and thereby saved the controls on crude-oil prices from total emasculation.

Some refiners process much greater proportions of old crude than others. In order to prevent these fortunate refiners from reaping vast windfall profits, the FEO had to enforce differential ceilings on the prices refiners could charge for their products. The method was to allow each refiner a specified markup over its full unit production costs. Even within well-defined geographical markets, the price controls on old crude led to intercompany differences of as much as 12¢ per gallon in retail gasoline prices.

All petroleum products were in short supply during the Arab embargo. Hence, even companies whose products carried prices as much as 20 percent above those of their competitors because they processed proportionately more of the high-priced new and foreign crude did not lose sales. However, once the embargo ended and the shortages eased, these companies confronted the dilemma of maintaining their prices and watching their sales plummet or cutting prices and incurring huge losses. This situation was neither "fair" nor economically desirable. However, given multi-tiered pricing for crude oil, the unhappy choice could be avoided only by requiring relatively

---

[26] See "NPRA Complains about Two-Tier Crude Pricing," *Oil and Gas Journal,* 24 September 1973, p. 82.

crude-rich refiners to sell (at controlled prices) some of their cheap crude to crude-short refiners. Disregarding the vigorous protests of the crude-rich refiners, who felt (correctly) that they were being asked to subsidize their less fortunate competitors, the FEO and its successor, the Federal Energy Administration, enforced the interrefinery allocation rules discussed earlier.

The Failure of Price Controls on Crude Oil. The foregoing discussion provides a taste of the complexities of the price regulations on crude oil and of the problems arising from their enforcement. The FEO was aware of most of these problems. It used much of its scarce manpower trying to make the controls more efficient and equitable and to enforce them properly, but to no avail. Unfortunately, because crude oil was in such short supply, inequities and inefficiencies were inherent in any system of effective price controls. Perhaps even worse than the myriad problems that the controls caused was their failure to achieve one of their main goals, restraint on profits.[27] To illustrate, in the first quarter of 1974, in the aftermath of the OAPEC decision to embargo oil sales, earnings of thirty of the largest U.S.-based oil companies soared 78.4 percent over the same period in 1973.[28]

The FEO never questioned the desirability of preventing the oil industry from reaping windfall profits due to the OAPEC embargo. Recognizing the need for voluntary public support for its energy conservation plans and the enormous public distrust of the oil industry, I concur with this decision. But controlling windfall profits is not without problems. Most important, it places the government in the difficult position of defining acceptable profit levels. Judged by the most common measure—the rate of return on equity investments—profits of most U.S. oil companies were below the average for all U.S. industry for the ten years prior to the OAPEC embargo.[29]

---

[27] Slowing inflation was the initial motivation of the Cost of Living Council for enforcing petroleum price controls. However, after the onslaught of the OAPEC embargo, the goal of preventing windfall profits assumed at least equal importance.

[28] "U.S. Oil Sees Possible Profit Slowdown," *Oil and Gas Journal*, 13 May 1974, pp. 40–41.

[29] A Federal Trade Commission report cited by the *Oil and Gas Journal*, 18 February 1974, p. 38, shows that, for the twelve months ending September 1973, oil refiners earned a return on equity of 10.5 percent compared with 12.4 percent for all U.S. manufacturing. Because the oil industry enjoys special tax treatment (the oil depletion allowance and quick expensing of many development costs), a comparison of unadjusted returns on equity may understate slightly the industry's profitability vis-à-vis other industries. However, it is unlikely that these adjustments would be sufficient to explain away the entire difference in average returns on equity.

When profits of twenty-five leading oil companies rose nearly 53 percent in 1973, their rate of return on equity was 15.1 percent against more than 14 percent for all U.S. manufacturing.[30] These comparisons do not establish that profits in the American oil industry were "excessive" and needed to be controlled.

The price controls failed to limit the post-embargo profits of oil companies for three reasons. First, the sharp rise in the price of foreign oil roughly doubled the value of stocks of foreign crude. Large inventory profits were realized when crude bought at pre-embargo world prices was sold at post-embargo prices. Price controls on domestically produced crude oil could not limit this source of approximately half of the higher profits attributable to the embargo. Second, because they did not wish to worsen shortages, the designers of the price controls exempted new, released, and stripper oil, which accounted for roughly 40 percent of all domestic crude. This was a wise decision. However, the shortage pushed prices of exempt domestic crude from less than $6.00 per barrel on the eve of the embargo to nearly $10.00 by late December; roughly three-fourths of the higher revenues due to this price rise accrued as higher profits to the owners of exempt crude.[31] Third, the FEO, wanting to maintain output in the face of escalating production costs, granted producers of old oil a price rise of $1.00 per barrel.

It should be stressed that the inefficiencies and inequities of price controls, and their ultimate failure to limit oil-company profits, were not the fault of the FEO. It made repeated attempts to remedy these deficiencies. Rather, the fault lies with the basic policy of controlling the price of a product at a level so low that its demand far exceeds its supply.[32]

A Remedy. The United States may experience renewed interruptions in oil supplies. In that event, it may once again seek to limit the profits of oil companies to gain public acceptance of the necessary austerity measures. The unsatisfactory experience with price controls

---

[30] See "Treasury Cites 1968–72 U.S. Profits Dip for Oil's Top 22," *Oil and Gas Journal*, 18 February 1974, pp. 38–39; and "Top Oil Firms 1973 Profits Jump 52.7%," *Oil and Gas Journal*, 18 February 1974, pp. 32–33.

[31] Royalties and severance taxes typically take up about 20 percent of any rise in oil revenues. Inflation-caused higher production costs probably ate up another 5 to 10 percent of the $4 hike in the price of exempt crude.

[32] The FEO also could have avoided several problems in gasoline allocation if there had been no petroleum price controls. For example, gasoline prices would have been relatively higher in the Northeast, giving refiners an incentive to eliminate regional disparities in supplies. Similarly, the FEO would not have had to adopt interrefinery allocation rules.

prompts me to suggest an alternative policy to meet any new crisis in petroleum supply. First, prices of crude oil and refined products should be allowed to rise freely both to discourage their consumption and to facilitate the allocation of scarce supplies to their most important uses. However, the government should have ready for quick implementation a rationing program designed to restrict demands to the supplies available—if, and only if, the petroleum shortage is so great that it threatens to push prices up to politically intolerable levels. Second, to prevent the oil companies from reaping windfall profits from crisis-bred higher prices, Congress should pass legislation that requires the President to impose a temporary excise tax on sales of petroleum products after a formal finding of an energy crisis by the Federal Energy Administration. (It is tempting to recommend the inclusion of a tax on excess profits in this legislation as an alternative presidential option. But I suspect that, as was the case with price controls recently, an efficient and equitable excess-profits tax is impossible to devise. Furthermore, in practice, companies find many ways to avoid this type of tax.) The temporary excise tax should be set nearly equal to the maximum hike in the prices of petroleum products that Congress feels Americans would tolerate under the circumstances. If Congress feels that poor Americans would suffer a disproportionate burden from a temporary petroleum excise tax, it should also require that its imposition be coupled with offsetting income tax credits or some other type of tax reduction.

4. The FEO's Staffing Problems

This paper has explained how many of the FEO's policies actually exacerbated the U.S. energy crisis. Should blame for the ultimate failure of these policies be placed on the FEO's leadership and staff?

The FEO was created after the energy crisis was already in full force. No well-considered plans awaited it, and from all sides—congressional, executive, and public—came urgent calls for bold new policies. Even a well-established agency can flounder in a crisis atmosphere. But FEO was brand new and was, of necessity, in the throes of a massive expansion.

In its new and still unsettled state, the agency especially needed strong day-to-day supervision from the top. Unfortunately, its two top officials—Administrator William Simon and Deputy Administrator John Sawhill—could not supply it because they had to spend most of their time testifying before congressional committees, pleading with various interest groups, or appealing directly to the American people to conserve energy.[33] Because Simon and Sawhill were nearly exhausted by these public relations activities, the direction of day-to-day operations was frequently left to seven assistant administrators and the general counsel. Most of these men were not accustomed to exercising such significant administrative power and responsibility. Several knew little about energy problems. In the absence of top-level leadership and of established decision-making traditions, these assistants and their nascent staffs inevitably spent considerable time jockeying for internal power.[34]

The FEO's rapid rate of growth also led to staffing problems at lower levels. Even after raids on other governmental agencies, few of the important staff positions were filled with people versed in petroleum matters. Almost no one on the staff had the first-hand experience in the oil industry that might have prevented FEO's complex pricing and allocation regulations from having their frequently undesirable consequences. The obvious way to remedy this particular staff weakness would have been to hire experienced people from the oil industry. However, because both Congress and the FEO's top leadership feared that such employees would unavoidably appear to have conflicts of interest, this alternative was not politically feasible.

In sum, the FEO did suffer severe staffing problems. Nevertheless, it would be fatuous to blame these for the ultimate failure of the FEO's regulations. Given the lack of preparation for dealing with any significant interruption in petroleum supply and the impossibility of insulating the FEO from the belligerent demands of politically powerful interest groups, severe staffing problems were unavoidable. In fact, taking account of the conditions under which the staff had to operate, I believe that it deserves high marks.[35]

5. Lessons

In addition to dramatizing the need for long-term policies to reduce U.S. dependence on insecure oil supplies, the largely unsuccessful

---

[33] Source: newspaper reports and interviews with former FEO officials.

[34] Source: interviews with former FEO officials.

[35] Other independent observers of the FEO appear to concur with this conclusion. For example, after attending the first meeting of the FEO's blue-ribbon Evaluation Panel on the Short-term Energy Situation, Walter Heller, chairman of the Council of Economic Advisers under President Kennedy, wrote in a letter (dated 5 January 1974): "With respect to personalities, both Simon and Sawhill make a very good impression. They were aware of the pitfalls in their data and in their public posture. As to the staff, their economists also made a good impression, but they are distinctly shorthanded for the huge job they have to do."

efforts of the FEO in the crisis of 1973–74 suggest four lessons for mitigating the impact should the nation become the target of another petroleum embargo.[36]

First, the Federal Energy Administration should not be swayed by shrill threats of the magnitude of the petroleum shortages in a new crisis. The embargoing countries have an obvious interest in exaggerating these cutbacks to induce swift and total compliance with their demands. The Federal Energy Administration must also carefully discount the exaggeration arising because each oil-importing country (and each interest group within that country) prepares for the worst by assuming—and claiming—that it will suffer especially severe interruptions. It is useful to remember that not *all* countries (and *all* interest groups) can suffer more than the average. Recent experience confirms that the FEO would have had a better appreciation of the real magnitude of the U.S. petroleum shortage if it had examined trends in oil inventories rather than relying on self-serving claims by the embargoers and domestic oil consumers, or on the too anxious predictions of its own staff.

Second, the Federal Energy Administration should declare publicly that, in future petroleum-supply crises, it will not adopt policies that prevent rising petroleum prices. Higher prices should be one of the administration's most powerful tools for obtaining necessary reductions in demand and for allocating scarce supplies to their most important uses. Assuming that Congress passes the appropriate enabling legislation, either excise taxes (or excess-profit taxes) should be used to prevent the oil companies from garnering higher profits from a petroleum embargo.

Third, every effort should be made now—in a crisis-free atmosphere that is favorable to careful design—to pass legislation that would allow the Federal Energy Administration promptly to implement rationing and taxing policies in a new emergency.

Fourth, to facilitate the third recommendation, the Federal Energy Administration should assign a small permanent staff to make ready to administer a comprehensive program of rationing should another embargo push oil prices to politically intolerable levels. Because any rationing system would be cumbersome to administer and would severely distort resource allocation, this plan should be implemented

---

[36] Several policies for eliminating U.S. dependence on insecure oil are discussed in Richard B. Mancke, *The Failure of U.S. Energy Policy* (New York: Columbia University Press, 1974), and in M.I.T. Energy Laboratory Policy Study Group, *Energy Self-Sufficiency: An Economic Evaluation* (Washington, D. C.: American Enterprise Institute, 1974).

only after the FEA has reached a formal finding of a likely supply interruption so large that no other policy will prove adequate for reducing demand quickly and sufficiently.

6. The Future of the Federal Energy Administration

U.S. energy policy has always emanated in bits and pieces from a variety of power centers. Prior to the establishment of the FEO, the most important were five executive departments—Interior, Treasury, State, Defense, and Commerce—and four administrative agencies or regulatory commissions—the Atomic Energy Commission, the Cost of Living Council, the Federal Power Commission, and the Environmental Protection Agency. Within many of these were several competing power centers, and all were subject, in varying degrees, to input from a plethora of congressional committees, presidential assistants, the Office of Management and Budget, the courts, industries, landowners, state governments, and the citizenry. By deliberate design as much as mere neglect, each of these power centers saw only a part of the total energy problem and each typically represented only a few of the legitimately concerned interests.[37]

Ideally, the Federal Energy Administration, the congressionally authorized successor to the FEO, should provide the coordination the United States needs for an effective and comprehensive energy policy. In actuality, because the major sources of U.S. energy policy making in the past have successfully defended their right to set policy in their historical bailiwicks, the creation of the new agency has not eliminated the problems stemming from a failure to coordinate U.S. energy policy. Instead, the mission of the Federal Energy Administration has been restricted to two principal concerns: running existing petroleum allocation programs and devising plans to achieve the amorphous goals of "Project Independence." Unless the scope of the Federal Energy Administration is expanded, it seems likely that U.S. energy policy will continue to languish for lack of coordination.

---

[37] For a more elaborate discussion of these problems, see Richard B. Mancke, "The Genesis of the U.S. Energy Crisis," in Joseph Szyliowicz and Bard O'Neill, eds., *The Energy Crisis and U.S. Foreign Policy* (New York: Praeger, forthcoming 1975).

Cover and book design: Pat Taylor

SELECTED 1974 PUBLICATIONS TO DATE

NATIONAL ENERGY STUDIES

U.S. ENERGY POLICY: A PRIMER, Edward J. Mitchell (103 pages, $3.00)

NATURAL GAS REGULATION: AN EVALUATION OF FPC PRICE CONTROLS, Robert B. Helms (84 pages, $3.00)

ENERGY SELF-SUFFICIENCY: AN ECONOMIC EVALUATION, M.I.T. Energy Laboratory Policy Study Group (89 pages, $3.00)

DIALOGUE ON WORLD OIL: HIGHLIGHTS OF A CONFERENCE ON WORLD OIL PROBLEMS (32 pages, $1.00)

DIALOGUE ON WORLD OIL, edited by Edward J. Mitchell (106 pages, paper $3.00, cloth $6.50)

THE NATURAL GAS SHORTAGE AND THE CONGRESS, Patricia E. Starratt (68 pages, $3.00)

PERFORMANCE OF THE FEDERAL ENERGY OFFICE, Richard B. Mancke (25 pages, $1.50)

OTHER STUDIES AND PROCEEDINGS

ARMS IN THE PERSIAN GULF, Dale R. Tahtinen (31 pages, $2.00)

THE ENERGY CRISIS, Paul W. McCracken, moderator (110 pages, $2.00)

PRIVATE FOUNDATIONS: BEFORE AND AFTER THE TAX REFORM ACT OF 1969, William H. Smith and Carolyn P. Chiechi (83 pages, $3.00)

REGULATION OF PHARMACEUTICAL INNOVATION: THE 1962 AMENDMENTS, Sam Peltzman (118 pages, $3.00)

FEDERAL TRANSIT SUBSIDIES: THE URBAN MASS TRANSPORTATION ASSISTANCE PROGRAM, George W. Hilton (131 pages, $3.00)

SIGNIFICANT DECISIONS OF THE SUPREME COURT, 1972-73 TERM, Bruce E. Fein (136 pages, $3.00)

THE FUTURE OF THE CHINA MARKET: PROSPECTS FOR SINO-AMERICAN TRADE, Edward Neilan and Charles R. Smith (94 pages, $3.00)

AGREEMENT ON BERLIN: A STUDY OF THE 1970-72 QUADRIPARTITE NEGOTIATIONS, Dennis L. Bark (131 pages, $3.00)

FOOD SAFETY REGULATION: A STUDY OF THE USE AND LIMITATIONS OF COST-BENEFIT ANALYSIS, Rita Ricardo Campbell (59 pages, $3.00)

ESSAYS ON INFLATION AND INDEXATION, Herbert Giersch, Milton Friedman, William Fellner, Edward M. Bernstein, Alexandre Kafka (98 pages, $3.00)

RESPONSIBLE PARENTHOOD: THE POLITICS OF MEXICO'S NEW POPULATION POLICIES, Frederick C. Turner (43 pages, $2.00)

THE HYDRA-HEADED MONSTER: THE PROBLEM OF INFLATION IN THE UNITED STATES, Phillip Cagan (59 pages, $3.00)

IS THE ENERGY CRISIS CONTRIVED? Paul W. McCracken, moderator (44 pages, $2.00)

INFLATION AND THE EARNING POWER OF DEPRECIABLE ASSETS, Eric Schiff (36 pages, $2.00)

WHAT PRICE DEFENSE?, Edmund S. Muskie and Bill Brock (73 pages, paper $2.50, cloth $5.75)

TOWARD A REALISTIC MILITARY ASSISTANCE PROGRAM, Robert J. Pranger and Dale R. Tahtinen (48 pages, $2.00)

BRAZIL AND THE UNITED STATES: TOWARD A MATURING RELATIONSHIP, Roger W. Fontaine (127 pages, $3.00)

OBSCENITY: THE COURT, THE CONGRESS AND THE PRESIDENT'S COMMISSION, Lane V. Sunderland (127 pages, $3.00)

Discounts: 25 to 99 copies—20%; 100 to 299 copies—30%;
300 to 499 copies—40%; 500 and over—50%

Performance of the Federal Energy Office by Richard B. Mancke seeks to evaluate the role played by the Federal Energy Office (FEO) during the oil embargo imposed by the members of the Organization of Arab Petroleum Exporting Countries (OAPEC). The FEO was established after the start of the OAPEC embargo and charged with the responsibility for initiating policies to alleviate the ill effects of the oil shortages that resulted from the OAPEC action. Initially, the most important task was to take steps to prevent the United States from running out of oil products. The FEO responded with several allocation measures aimed at closing the oil-supply gap by reducing U.S. demands in an equitable way. It also enforced price controls. The author concludes that, on balance, the FEO's allocation measures and price controls not only exacerbated U.S. oil-supply problems but failed to create a more equitable distribution of the embargo's costs. From this probe of the underlying causes of the FEO's policy failures, the most important lesson that emerges concerns planning. Prior to the OAPEC embargo, the United States government had only the vaguest plans for dealing with such a contingency. Thus, both Congress and the White House panicked when it occurred. Good decision making is at best difficult in such a crisis atmosphere. It becomes nearly impossible when the organization responsible for making speedy decisions lacks adequate staff, administrative traditions, and a well-defined decision-making hierarchy, and is subject to political pressures from a plethora of interest groups—as was the case with the FEO.

Richard B. Mancke is associate professor of international economic relations at the Fletcher School of Law and Diplomacy, Tufts University.

$1.50

 American Enterprise Institute for Public Policy Research
1150 Seventeenth Street, N.W., Washington, D. C. 20036